CITY DOG COUNTRY DOG

Sally Harding is a photographer and journalist who lives in the Adelaide Hills with her partner, their two children and a retired guide dog. Her work has featured in newspapers, magazines and calendars and is known for its humour and personality.

The collection of photographic images for *City Dog Country Dog* first began when she was a child playing around with dogs and cameras, both of which have become lifelong friends.

CITY DOG
COUNTRY DOG

SALLY HARDING

Wakefield
Press

Wakefield Press
1 The Parade West
Kent Town
South Australia 5067
www.wakefieldpress.com.au

First published 2010
Reprinted 2011

Photography by Sally Harding et al
Design by Kieran Hooper
Printing and quality control in China by Tingleman Pty Ltd

National Library of Australia Cataloguing-in-Publication entry

Author: Harding, Sally, 1971–   .
Title: City dog country dog/Sally Harding.
ISBN: 978 1 86254 915 9 (pbk.).
Subjects: Dogs – Australia.
                 Dogs – Effect of human beings on.
                 Human–animal relationships – Australia.
Dewey Number: 636.70994

Introduction

Despite its title, *City Dog Country Dog* doesn't aim to pigeonhole dogs into two simple categories. Funnily enough, it's quite the opposite.

Its purpose is to show the adaptability, loyalty and unconditional love that dogs provide. In cities, suburbs or in the middle of nowhere, our home is their home – no questions asked. And dogs will happily work all day to earn their keep, then sleep on the floor at night if that's all they're given. Fortunately, though, the sleeping conditions for most Australian dogs are much better.

The inspiration behind this book is an old Aesop fable: 'The City Mouse and the Country Mouse'. In the story, a city mouse and his country cousin swap lives to see which they prefer. In the end, they both cherish what they already have.

This theme of swapping between extremities has inspired a colourful pictorial essay about Australian lifestyle, and never before have photographic subjects been so easy to find or people so willing to go out of their way to assist!

Although I've been slobbered on, howled at and even humped, I must say that working with the 60 or so dogs featured in this book has been an absolute pleasure. I still can't put into words why I like dogs so much. Perhaps that's why I photograph them instead.

A very special thank you to fellow photographic contributors Nicole Clare Emanuel, David Highet and Stefanie Mellon, but especially to my quasi pictorial editor Grant Nowell, who is a wonderful human being, photographer and mentor.

SALLY HARDING

The Lions Hearing Dogs Training Centre

At least twice a month the manager of the Lions Hearing Dogs Training Centre receives a letter from a hearing-impaired client somewhere in Australia, telling him their dog has done something extraordinary.

'I can't tell you the number of times these dogs have saved an owner's life,' says Bill Holmes, Centre Manager. 'One client was recently overcome by fumes when a column oil heater caught fire. Her dog brought her around by persistent licking.'

There are so many other extraordinary things to tell about hearing dogs, yet this Adelaide Hills organisation that trains and donates hundreds of these clever-thinking dogs is the underdog of both the charity and dog-service worlds.

Hearing dogs are trained to respond to a variety of auditory cues, including baby cries, door knocks and bells, smoke alarms, ringing telephones, SMS alerts and other everyday sounds. The dogs 'work' by locating the source of the sound, making physical contact with their owner, and leading them to the source of the sound. They are often taught simple sign language, too, and undergo basic obedience to conduct themselves well in public, where they are granted legal access to all areas.

The Lions Hearing Dogs Training Centre is one of the few service charities in Australia that sources most of its animals from death row at pet shelters, never relinquishing unsuitable dogs ('lovable dropouts') to anything less than a wonderful home. Potential candidates come in all shapes and sizes, so even the short, scruffy and not-so-pretty dogs aren't left behind.

Furthermore, the Lions Hearing Dogs Training Centre is one of only a few accredited hearing-dog organisations in the southern hemisphere. It operates with just a handful of staff who work a shoestring budget mostly funded by the Lions Clubs of Australia, Papua New Guinea and Norfolk Island, and other loyal sponsors.

Part-proceeds from sales of this book will be donated to the centre, so it can continue its magnificent work improving the independence and lifestyle of the hearing-impaired.

For further information or to make a donation:

Lions Hearing Dogs Inc.
PO Box 164
Hahndorf SA 5245 Australia
Ph: +61 8 8388 7836
Fax: 61 8 8388 1299
TTY: +61 8 8388 1297
www.hearingdogs.asn.au

HEARING DOGS are identified by their bright orange leads and collars. Some also wear an orange jacket or harness.
Photo © Jeremy Watson

Foreword

I love it when a carload of city friends arrives at the farm. Almost always there's a dog or two – lovely, well-mannered dogs; clean, groomed dogs; dogs who know the ways of the civilised world, who know their macchiatos from their cappuccinos, who come when they're called and offer a dainty paw as a greeting.

Swooped on, overwhelmed with rustic enthusiasm by our team, greeted with yipping, wheel-pissing delight, these urbane and refined creatures of the cosmopolitan world, not unreasonably, tuck their tails and retreat behind their owners' legs. But not for long: a rambunctious, irreverent farm welcome wins every time. Our uncouth canine hosts cut through snobby conformism and, before long, genteel white-haired lap dogs and workaholic kelpies are doing fly-pasts together with stupid grins on their faces. While humans more quietly break down cultural barriers with a glass of red at sunset, these vulgar rurals teach their city mates that rolling in fresh manure and rotting carcasses cuts the language divide superbly, and gets a fantastic reaction from the audience.

A day without a dog would be bleak. There's one on the back of my quad bike, or at my feet while I write, a tail flapping encouragingly as I talk through sentences out loud. The kitchen on a winter's day has dogs warming paws in front of the wood stove. Under the pine trees, the working dog waits to be summoned.

A dog with country genes was my companion during my single days in the city. Bred to muster sheep, she adapted well to suburbia – charming pies from the baker and sausages from the butcher while I was at work. She then taught me the joys of country living when farming became my new life.

When our fox-hunting, rat-catching, hooligan terriers have occasionally had city holidays, we notice how they adopt the reverential, eye-flapping gestures of cultured society. Astonishingly, they sit quietly beneath the café table and lap politely at the communal water bowl.

That's the wonderful thing about dogs. They are versatile, happy to do and be whatever we want of them. But at their heart they are all just dogs, and pleased to have us as their pack leaders.

While we can't help but admire the job evolution has done on the wolf prototype, it's altogether another matter to capture the many moods and guises of our favourite companions on camera, but what a brilliant photographic essay Sally Harding has produced! Each sparkling shot affirms the talents of dogs at being mind-readers, comfort-givers, comedians, admirers of our genius, as well as sometimes being pretty jolly useful.

Thank you dogs, you make the mundane into an adventure!

ANGELA GOODE
Journalist, farmer and author of *Great Australian Working Dog Stories* (Harper Collins), and *Great Working Horse Stories* (Allen & Unwin).

A city mouse once went on a visit to his cousin in the country.
He was rough and ready, this country cousin, but he
loved his city cousin and made him heartily welcome . . .

'The City Mouse and the Country Mouse' – Aesop

CUTE AS A BUTTON
A Maltese cross hits the
streets in high fashion

SHOWING OFF
Bichon Frise show dogs with perfectly
manicured hairstyles

GOOD JOB
A farmer praises kelpies
Kimba and Choco

OUT IN FORCE
Dog owners take part in a fundraising
walk for a local animal shelter

END OF THE DAY
A kelpie does his final
boundary check for the day

DOG FACT

There are over four million dogs in Australia, half of which are crossbreeds. On average one in every three households has a dog. South Australia and the Northern Territory have the highest dog proportion, with 20 dogs for every 100 people, compared to the national average of 18.

BIG LOVE
Jonas Moham-Wild sees eye to eye with Filou, a 90 kg Great Dane

GETTING TIRED
Knockabout terriers Tally and
Spud wait for their master

NO TIME TO WAIT
Hound puppies Paper
and Pencil rip it up

UP CLOSE AND PERSONAL
Borzoi show dogs, Rusty and Nina

KEEPING A CLOSE EYE
Australian shepherds, Fynn and Smudge

DOG FACT

Australia's most recognised dog breeds are the kelpie, Australian cattle dog, Australian stumpy tail cattle dog, Australian terrier, Australian silky terrier and Tenterfield terrier. The German koolie is also Australian, however the Australian shepherd originated in the United States.

DINKY-DI AUSSIES
An Australian cattle dog and its kelpie mate enjoy a run in the sun

London

Standard Poodle

OWNERS
Michelle and David Auld

HAPPIEST WHEN
I'm all wet and scruffy at the beach.
I also like eating very much!

FAVOURITE PLACE TO SLEEP
In the bedroom with my owners

GREATEST ACHIEVEMENT
Being dyed bright colours to be the star
attraction at a pet expo

MOST LOVABLE TRAIT
I tilt my head to the side when
I don't understand something

Darwin
(Northern Territory)

CITY DOG

Pictures supplied by Michelle Auld

Millie

Koolie

OWNERS
Zoe Phillips and Stuart Thege

HAPPIEST WHEN
Playing fetch. I'll fetch anything

FAVOURITE PLACE TO SLEEP
On my owners' bed on a Saturday morning
(the only day dogs are allowed)

GREATEST ACHIEVEMENT
An uncanny understanding of spoken English

MOST LOVABLE TRAIT
I'm very athletic and I'll jump onto
anything you ask

Lancefield
(Victoria)

Pictures supplied by Zoe Phillips

TOUGH LOVE
Scott Maney takes a break from
work to spend time with Turbo, an
American Staffordshire bull terrier

DOG FACT

Certain dog breeds are restricted
and banned in some Australian
states and territories. The most
widely affected breeds are the
American pit bull terrier, Dogo
Argentino, Fila Brasileiro and the
Japanese Toso. It is estimated
there are over 100,000 dog bites
each year, with two out of every
three bites involving the family,
neighbour or friend's pet dog 'in
the backyard'. No dog breed in
particular is held accountable
for these attacks. (Source: Delta
Society Australia)

LITTLE BUDDIES
Basil the Jack Russell terrier sticks
close to baby Angus Bilsborow

WARM COMPANY
A boy and his kelpie huddle up
against the winter chills

CAFÉ DOG
Murphy the cairn terrier
out socialising with his
owner, Diana Pedrick

WAITING IN LINE
Peg the border collie tags along to
a sheepdog trial with competition
dogs, Pye and Chips

DOG FACT

There are over 300 official place names in Australia that include the word 'dog'. These include: Native Dog Beach, Western Australia; Mount Wild Dog, South Australia; Dead Dog Waterhole, Northern Territory; Dog Leg Lagoon, Queensland; Shaggy Dog Ridge, New South Wales; Dog Island, Victoria; and Dog Bark, Tasmania.

FRIENDSHIP WITHOUT BORDERS
Toddler Kelly Hooper gets to know Tju-Tju, a camp dog originally from Central Australia

A BIT OF BLING
A chihuahua contestant at the annual Doggywood
dog show at Sydney's Gay and Lesbian Mardi Gras

WORK WEAR
Sheepdogs wear muzzles if they tend
to nip stock while mustering

A GENTLE HAND
Lucas Pantano, 4, shares a quiet
moment with Charlie the Jack
Russell terrier/Maltese crossbreed

COUNTRY LANE
Robbie the bearded collie
accompanies his family
on a Sunday walk

TAKEN FOR A RIDE
A pair of golden labradors
on a shopping trip

DOG FACT

Animal welfare laws require
dogs to be restrained on the
back of a moving open-top
vehicle or utility, unless they
are droving stock. For dogs
travelling inside a car it is also
advised to use a harness that
attaches to seat belts.

Kiiara

Siberian Husky

OWNERS
Michelle and Marc Warwick

HAPPIEST WHEN
I'm off-lead and running free

FAVOURITE PLACE TO SLEEP
Under the air-conditioning vent in summer
or in a backyard burrow I dug myself

GREATEST ACHIEVEMENT
Being an all-round good sport and
competing in obedience, agility, flyball
and endurance trials

MOST LOVABLE TRAIT
I make you earn my affection,
so you know it's for real!

CITY DOG

Canberra
(ACT)

Pictures supplied by the Warwick family

Anna

Hungarian Vizsla

OWNERS
Toby and Sue Crockett

HAPPIEST WHEN
I'm keeping my owners company

FAVOURITE PLACE TO SLEEP
Deep under the duvet on the human
bed in the horse truck

GREATEST ACHIEVEMENT
Surviving a brutal attack from a goanna
I chased in the garden. I still chase
goannas though!

MOST LOVABLE TRAIT
Protecting our free-range chooks from any
other dogs that may cause them harm

COUNTRY DOG

Fernvale
(Queensland)

Pictures supplied by the Crockett family

DOG FACT

The top ten most common pet dog names in Australia are Max, Jessie, Molly, Sam, Jack, Chloe, Bonnie, Lucy, Jake and Toby. Other popular names include Red, Blue, Rusty, Lady, Monty, Diesel, Bundy, Scruffy and Mate.

FLAT-OUT
Mate, an ageing Rottweiler crossbreed, takes a nap on the back verandah of a country homestead

PERFECT COUPLE
Keeshound show dogs
Boston and Hope

MOTLEY CREW
Koolie sheepdogs
Patch and Meg

RELAXED AND HAPPY
Onyx Taylor with her dogs, Bradley the
schnauzer and Ishtah, a Shiba Inu

ONE TRICK PONY
Olympic equestrian rider Megan Jones with
her dog, Jackie the Jack Russell terrier

DOG FACT

Australia's most popular purebred pet dog choices include the Maltese, Jack Russell terrier, poodle, Staffordshire bull terrier, Australian cattle dog, kelpie, border collie, labrador retriever, golden retriever and German shepherd.

CITY DOG

A DOG'S BREAKFAST
Lady the whippet accompanies her owners while they enjoy an alfresco brunch

DRINK BREAK
Dogs gather around a watering
station at a city off-leash dog park

FRESHENING UP
Farm dogs pile into a cattle watering
trough to drink and cool off

NATURALLY NOSEY
Pound dogs Monty and Benny hope
it's their turn to be re-homed

OVER HERE
Lily the whippet watches
from behind the farm gate

DOGS IN A LOG
A dingo and her pup
take shelter in a fallen
gum tree trunk

DOG FACT

The scientific name for dingoes is
Canis lupus dingo, which means
wolf with a dingo difference.
Although they are considered
Australia's native dog it is believed
they were introduced around 4000
years ago by Asian seafarers.
Pioneer farmers protected sheep
from the wild dog by erecting what
is now called The Dingo Fence –
5614 km of wire fencing stretching
from Queensland to southern
western Australia.

Devo

Whippet

OWNER
Phoebe Clarence

HAPPIEST WHEN
I'm on holidays with my family

FAVOURITE PLACE TO SLEEP
Curled in my own bed

GREATEST ACHIEVEMENT
Being a fun-loving and affectionate dog

MOST LOVABLE TRAIT
Getting so hyped up I don't watch where
I'm going (I once ran straight into a wall!)

CITY DOG

Sunbury
(Victoria)

Pictures supplied by the Clarence family

Wilbur

Australian Cattle Dog

OWNER
Nicky Read

HAPPIEST WHEN
It's windy so I can chase the leaves

FAVOURITE PLACE TO SLEEP
I keep chewing up my bedding so
it's usually on the grass

GREATEST ACHIEVEMENT
I toss and catch my own toys

MOST LOVABLE TRAIT
I'll always find a way to get where I want
to be . . . even if it means climbing ladders!

COUNTRY DOG

Paraburdoo
(Western Australia)

Pictures supplied by Nicky Read and Catherine Blake

CITY DOG

TOP DOG
Once a neglected and frightened puppy, Hugo the dalmatian now enjoys the high life with new owner Joshua Heath

DOG FACT

Famous Australian literary dogs include 'The Loaded Dog' by poet Henry Lawson, and the dog who sat on the tucker box 'Nine Miles From Gundagai' by poet Jack Moses. Stars of the screen include Kane, a well-known blue cattle dog in TV commercials, the labrador character Bouncer in *Neighbours* and the oversized costumed dog Wags from The Wiggles.

OFFICE DOG
Web designer Nick Riley enjoys the company of a colleague's
dog, Fraser the Weimaraner. The office has an 'open dog'
policy allowing employees to bring their dogs to work

DRILLING DOG
Ellie the border collie often accompanies owner
Rick Walsh and his crew on months-long bore-sinking
expeditions to the Outback in search of water

IN HIGH PLACES
Police dog Riggs jumps an
agility obstacle with ease

UP AND OVER
A closed gate is no obstacle for a
kelpie on duty in the sheep yards

DOG FACT

Wise farmers say you can never have enough good dogs. A smart and efficient working dog will not only slash the amount of man-hours needed to move stock, it also improves occupational health and safety by keeping farmers away from the hooves of panicking beasts.

A CATTLEMAN AND HIS POSSE
Chris Hocking returns from a morning's mustering with dogs Danny, Sooty, One, Ted and Matey

BLUE-EYED BABY
Furgee, a young Australian bulldog. One or two blue
eyes is a feature of several other breeds, including the
Australian shepherd, koolie, Great Dane and dalmatian

TRUE-BLUE DOG
Ollie, a blue Australian cattle dog.
The breed was once nicknamed
Hall's heelers or Timmins biters

ALL ABOARD
Grazier Angus McLachlan and
his two kelpies Eddie and Solo
on the move

A QUICK DIP
Ignacio Mackinlay teaches
Scruffy the Jack Russell
terrier how to ride a board

NICE TO MEET YOU
Robbie the bearded collie
makes a new friend

DOG FACT

Australia's two most famous
dog statues are the Dog On
the Tuckerbox at Snake Gully
in New South Wales and a
memorial to a legendary roving
kelpie called Red Dog, located
in Dampier, Western Australia.

Leon

English Springer Spaniel

OWNER
Lesli Cameron

HAPPIEST WHEN
I'm carrying my favourite squeaky
toy around in my mouth

FAVOURITE PLACE TO SLEEP
On the couch next to my owner and dog brother, Kyte

GREATEST ACHIEVEMENT
Teaching my little sister Scout how to use a doggy door!

MOST LOVABLE TRAIT
When I was a puppy I was so plump I had to lie
down to eat . . . now I'm a top agility dog

Canberra
(ACT)

Pictures supplied by Lara Sedgmen

Jillian

Dachshund Crossbreed

OWNER
Lena Shephard

HAPPIEST WHEN
My owner comes home (if she hasn't taken me with her)

FAVOURITE PLACE TO SLEEP
In a basket next to my owner's bed

GREATEST ACHIEVEMENT
Surviving life as a stray before becoming a Lions Hearing Dog

MOST LOVABLE TRAIT
I run around in circles waiting for my dinner

COUNTRY DOG

Adelaide Hills
(South Australia)

DOG FACT

There are an estimated 80,000 working dogs in Australia, 98% of which are sheep and farm dogs. Other working dogs include guard dogs, assistance dogs, guide dogs, hearing dogs, police dogs, customs dogs and dogs used for pet therapy.

TRADIE DOG
Plumber Chris Mariner with his work companion and best buddy, Bonnie the kelpie

BLOWN AWAY
Paco the Pomeranian holds his
ground at the dog grooming salon

THE STAND-OFF
A stubborn sheep turns to face
a kelpie during a yard dog trial

TAKING STOCK
A kelpie sheepdog races off
to yard-up another mob

IN FROM THE SEA
Gil the wire-haired fox terrier proudly
retrieves a stick from the water

PUPPY LOVE
Tilly Gray, 7, with a litter of six-week-old Jack Russell terrier puppies

DOG FACT

Dog owners have a lower risk of cardiovascular disease and lower levels of cholesterol. Owning a dog also promotes an active and healthy lifestyle and provides many other psychological benefits. (Source: Baker Medical Research Institute, Melbourne)

SMALL BUT MIGHTY
Hungarian vizsla puppy Hester
pulls her weight around the farm

GENTLE GIANTS
Wolfhounds Gus and Rowan take
owner Jeannine Hooper for a walk

READY AND WILLING
Australian terrier Biggles
with kennel-mate, George
the labrador

OLD FARM DOG
Midgey the 14-year-old
kelpie with much-younger
Buddy, a koolie

DOG FACT

English settlers introduced foxes to Australia in the 1800s to continue the sport of hunting (with hounds) on horseback. The wild fox population thrived and is now considered one of the country's biggest threats to livestock and native wildlife.

POCKET ROCKETS
Jack Russell terriers in full flight during a fox hunting club terrier race

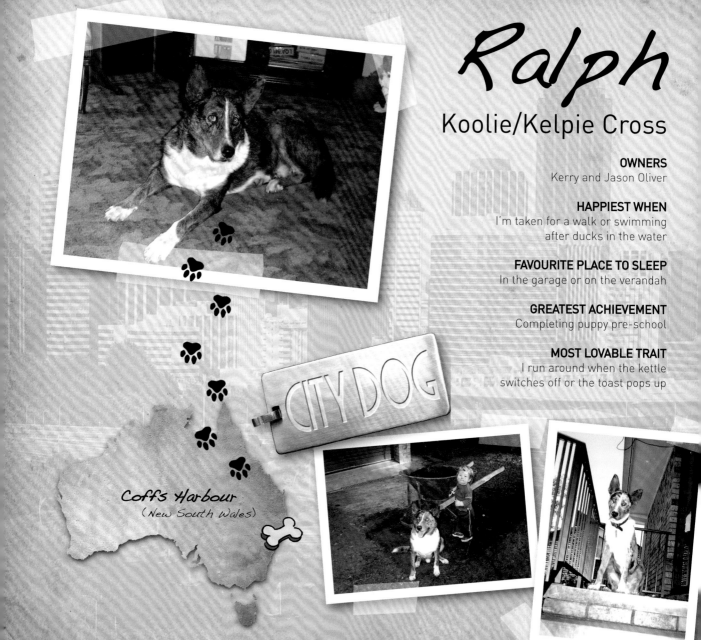

Ralph
Koolie/Kelpie Cross

OWNERS
Kerry and Jason Oliver

HAPPIEST WHEN
I'm taken for a walk or swimming
after ducks in the water

FAVOURITE PLACE TO SLEEP
In the garage or on the verandah

GREATEST ACHIEVEMENT
Completing puppy pre-school

MOST LOVABLE TRAIT
I run around when the kettle
switches off or the toast pops up

CITY DOG

Coffs Harbour
(New South Wales)

Pictures supplied by the Oliver family

Shaka

Rhodesian Ridgeback

OWNERS
Skye and Callum MacLachlan

HAPPIEST WHEN
My owners come home. I greet them with an enormous howl

FAVOURITE PLACE TO SLEEP
When I'm allowed I curl up beside my owners' bed . . . and snore all night

GREATEST ACHIEVEMENT
Saving a kelpie farm dog by barking and alerting everyone that she was trapped down a well

MOST LOVABLE TRAIT
Tapping on the window with my paw to ask to be let inside

COUNTRY DOG

Williamstown
(South Australia)

Pictures supplied by the MacLachlan family

BIG LEGS, LITTLE LEGS
Philipp Lischke takes Max
the dachshund for a jog along
Sydney's foreshore

DOG FACT

Dogs are legally required to be
walked on a leash in most cities,
except at designated leash-
free parks and beaches. Even
in the country it is advisable
to keep dogs under effective
control – not only are they a
threat to wildlife but they are at
risk themselves from fox bait,
crocodiles, snakes, paralysis
ticks and poisonous cane toads.

WIND IN YOUR HAIR
Sting the Old English sheepdog
prefers open-air travel

BEST SEAT IN TOWN
Dusty the kelpie keeps an eye on
things from his owner's stock truck

RIGHT BACK AT YOU
Nyuma the cavoodle (cavalier
King Charles spaniel x poodle)
fetches the ball

OBSESSIVE COMPULSIVE
Molly the border collie
satisfies her urge to chase
sheep with a tennis ball

DOG FACT

There are several locally
developed Australian dog
breeds, although they are not
always officially recognised.
These include the kangaroo
dog (a type of lurcher), the
Murray River curly coated
retriever, several pig hunting
dogs including the bull
Arab and the camp dog, a
hardy mixed breed from
central Australia.

FOUR-LEGGED FRIENDS
Polly the kangaroo dog
gets up close with Jack,
a Friesian crossbreed horse,
both owned by Jackie Boyd

CUTE AND CUDDLY
Tilda Thege, 3, and her
pal Budsy, a bull mastiff
crossbreed

UP IN ARMS
Australian champion standard
poodle, Remykn Don't Call Me Crazy
(aka Llewis), ringside at a dog show

GRABBING A NAP
A couple of farm dogs asleep
on the back of a ute

PAMPERED POOCHES
West highland terriers Colin
and Lacey lounging around

WHAT ABOUT ME?
Rueben the boxer anxiously
waiting for his owners to
return home

DOG FACT

Melbourne is ranked as the
most liveable city in Australia
for keeping a pet dog,
according to a survey by the
Australian Companion Animal
Council. The criteria include
the ability to keep a dog in a
residential dwelling, access to
parks and beaches, and the
amount of designated off-leash
areas. Adelaide came a close
second, with Perth third.

Wallace

Griffon Brussels

OWNER
Emily Kawalilak

HAPPIEST WHEN
Getting love, giving love or thinking about love

FAVOURITE PLACE TO SLEEP
Snuggled up to a warm body – human, dog, cat, whatever . . .

GREATEST ACHIEVEMENT
Avoiding my dog bed. My owner's bed is much better!

MOST LOVABLE TRAIT
The way my whole body wags when I'm excited

Sydney
(New South Wales)

Buster

Tenterfield Terrier

OWNERS
Mark and Sharon Thurston

HAPPIEST WHEN
I'm splashing in the water and chasing
the droplets

FAVOURITE PLACE TO SLEEP
Anything that belongs to my family –
towels, blankets, even the barbecue cover

GREATEST ACHIEVEMENT
Fathering a litter of four adorable puppies

MOST LOVABLE TRAIT
I have a really cute yawn and an
even better smile

COUNTRY DOG

Tintinara
(South Australia)

Pictures supplied by the Thurston family

DOG FACT

The oldest Aussie dog on record is an Australian cattle dog called Bluey from Rochester, Victoria, born on 7 June 1910 and living for 29 years, 5 months and 7 days. In 1984, however, a dog owner from Broadbeach, Queensland, claimed his Australian cattle dog/ labrador crossbreed, Chilla, beat this record by passing away at age 32. Neither of these claims have been verified by the Guinness World Records, but if correct, would make them the two oldest dogs in the world.

BOUNDING INTO THE SUNSET
An energetic terrier soaks up every last minute of daylight

OUT FOR THE COUNT
A seven-week-old Jack Russell terrier
puppy asleep on its owner's shoe

'Goodbye, Cousin,' said the country mouse.
'What! going so soon?' said the city mouse.
'Yes,' he replied, 'better beans and bacon in peace
than cakes and ale in fear.'

'The City Mouse and the Country Mouse' – Aesop

Acknowledgements

They say to never work with animals for a reason: it can be pretty jolly tricky. Consequently there is a very long list of people to thank for making this challenging task not just possible, but a heap of fun.

Firstly, a very big thank you to the following people for allowing themselves and/or their dogs to be photographed:
Wayne and Pamela Abra (Peg, Pye and Chips); Ben Attwood and Sara Mitchell (Hester); Megan Bennett (Rueben); Ollie Bevan and Stephanie Johnston (Gil); Angus, Ben and Lisa Bilsborow (Basil); Jackie Boyd (Tally, Spud and Polly); Laura Climatiamos (Paco); Kay D'Angelo (Lily); Robyn Davidson (Rusty); James Garvan and Clementine Johnson (Nyuma); Tilly, Andrew and Corri Gray (Hounds); Christabel and Bob Gurr (Kimba and Choco); Hahndorf Interim Animal Shelter (Benny and Monty); Joshua Heath and Sam Rice (Hugo); Tim Hill (Mate); Shirley and Chris Hocking (Danny, Sooty, One, Ted and Matey); Jeannine Hooper (Gus and Rowan); Kelly Hooper, Claire and James Cooper (Tju-Tju); Megan Jones (Jackie); John and Christine Kellow (Bichon Frise dogs); Tricia and Steve Kelm (Meg and Patch); Ollie Klein, Jeni Watson and Nick Riley (Fraser); Philipp Lischke and Christian Skaar (Max); Scott Maney (Turbo); Chris and Sue Mariner (Bonnie, Midgie and Buddy); Ignacio Mackinlay, Liz and Chris Addams Williams (Scruffy); Angus McLachlan (Solo and Eddie); Lesley and Fiona Mackness (Colin and Lacey); Nadine and John Mellor (Boston and Hope); Jonas Moham-Wild (Filou); Jenny Molloy (Ollie and Fly); Margie Nottle-Justice and Erin Carter's legs (Llewis); Lucas, Karen and Michael Pantano (Charlie); Diana Pedrick (Murphy); Nicola Portis (Furgee); Sam and Andrew Rammell (Lady); Tracey and Rory Rogers (Smudge and Fynn); James and Julie Sexton (Molly); Susie Smith (Biggles and George); SAPOL Sergeant Nicci Lycett and Senior Constable First Class Neil Stevenson (PD Riggs); Strath Stock Transport (Dusty); Sydney Gay and Lesbian Mardi Gras/Doggywood dog show (chihuahua); Onyx Taylor (Bradley and Ishtah); Tilda and Aaron Thege and Nicole Emanuel (Budsy); Irene Valli and Tom Moon (Sting); Rick Walsh (Ellie); Lyn and Peter Watson, Dingo Discovery Centre (dingo and pup); Gail Wood (Nina).

The following contributors kindly dug deep into their photo albums for personal photographs and fun facts about their dogs for the profile pages:
Michelle and David Auld (London); Lesli Cameron (Leon); Phoebe Clarence (Devo); Sue and Toby Crockett (Anna); Emily Kawalilak (Wallace); Skye and Callum MacLachlan (Shaka); Kerry and Jason Oliver (Ralph); Nicky Read (Wilbur); Lena Shephard (Jillian); Zoe Phillips and Stuart Thege (Millie); Sharon and Mark Thurston (Buster); Michelle and Marc Warwick (Kiiara).

CITY DOG COUNTRY DOG

A string of unbelievably generous doggy and non-doggy professionals stepped in to help with invaluable time and advice:
Max Anderson; Phil Astley, Plastyk Studios; Shaun Berg Lawyers; Trevor Drogemuller, PKF Accounting; Sandy Geci, The Sassy Dog; Mikyla Gilbert, *Adelaide Hills Magazine*; Angela Goode; Great Dane Association of NSW; Sarah Harris, Dog and Cat Management Board of South Australia; Margaret and Jeff Highet; Micil and Linda Knight, Alice's Kitchen; Jenny Lamattina; Sharon Myers; Mick Nolan; Craig Osborne; Ian Osterman and Andrew Kelleher, *The Courier*; Luiza Ziembicki and Bill Holmes, The Lions Hearing Dogs Training Centre.

A big thank you to the friends and family who encouraged me to stop dreaming and finally start photographing a dog book. My mother Jutta Rooney and sister Jane Jenkins for taking care of the children; gal-pals Sara Mitchell, Jacquie Sprott and Jo Papargiris for their loyalty, support and big hearts; dog lovers and all-round good guys Robyn Pine, Jenny Molloy, Tess O'Callaghan, Carolyn Mehrfert and Deb Painter.

But the biggest thank you of all goes to my darling partner, Kieran, who not only put this lovely book together but who works tirelessly night after night in front of a computer screen to keep our family ticking along during the day. We see what you do for us and we appreciate everything. Thank you.

Wakefield Press is an independent publishing and
distribution company based in Adelaide, South Australia.
We love good stories and publish beautiful books.
To see our full range of titles, please visit our website at
www.wakefieldpress.com.au.